I Believe In the Name of Jesus

Knowing Jesus through His Seven "I Am" Statements

By
Marjie Schaefer

This Bible study is affectionately dedicated to the prayer warriors who have been on the 'front lines' with me each step of the way and throughout the years.

These are women who know their Power Source and are dedicated to seeking Him daily and are faithful to cry out to Him on behalf of their sisters. These 'worshipping warriors' and dear friends are a life-line for me and all of the women of our Flourish community who they cover in prayer each week.

With profound gratitude and with great thanks to our Father for you:

Patricia Sieh

Gretchen Dillon

Leslye Hebert

Sherrie Snyder

Patti Heindel

What's in a name?

There is one name that equips and prepares us to live the lives we are destined and called to live. Names have implications and meaning. It is rare to ever get to know someone deeply and personally without learning their name.

How much more important then, for us to get to know Jesus through His Names? The power behind the Name of Jesus enables us to reach our divinely appointed destinations in life.

I believe we are living in critical days. Our world is rapidly changing, and we never know from one day to the next what or who will appear on the world stage. It is an exciting time to be alive and it is important for us to note that we were born for such a time as this!

The Lord has told us in His Word that He is the One who never changes. The world may be at a tipping point, but we are safe and secure in the everlasting arms of Jesus Christ!

Jesus made seven profound statements about who He is and what He is for us. These seven identity statements, or names, reveal life-changing implications for us.

In this study, we will take seven weeks to examine His seven "I Am" statements:

Jesus is the Light of the World—this is His radiance that reveals His loving Father, and through His light, we gain spiritual understanding and wisdom for living.

Jesus is the Bread of Life—He is our spiritual nourishment and the One who spiritually sustains us.

Jesus is the Door—Jesus has given us free and unlimited access to His Father and His Kingdom.

Jesus is the Good Shepherd—Jesus cares for us and has paid our entry fee into the Kingdom with His life.

Jesus is the Resurrection and the Life—Death could not hold Jesus; He has guaranteed our eternal life with God.

Jesus is the Way, the Truth, and the Life—Jesus is the map, the road, and the destination.

Jesus is the True Vine---Jesus is our connection to the Source of all of life.

We have so much to learn from Jesus as we begin to study these seven expressions of His names.

I love the story in John 6 where we see Jesus teaching the crowds of people and they are hanging on to His every word.

At one point they ask Him, "What are we to do, so that we may habitually be doing the works of God?"

I love the answer Jesus gives them, "This is the work of God: that you believe in the One whom He has sent." (John 6: 28-29)

This is so encouraging for us! From His statement, it seems to me that Jesus is not concerned with how much we do or how much we know..... He wants us to believe in Him.

The way that we grow in our faith and belief of Him is to get into His Word, study Him, learn His names, and embrace His teaching because faith comes by hearing, and hearing by the Word of God.

I am praying that we glean a greater revelation of who Jesus is as we work through this study. Having a fresh revelation for these days we live in, is what will empower us and equip us to shine brightly for Him and to help others live for Him too!

Together with Him,
Marjie

"I was regretting the past and fearing the future. Suddenly, my Lord was speaking: "*My Name is I am*". "When you live in the past with its mistakes and regrets, it is hard. I am not there. My name is not *I Was*. When you live in the future, with its problems and fear, it is hard. I am not there. My name is not *I Will Be*. When you live in this moment, it is not hard. I am here. *My name is I am!*"

~Helen Mallicoat (source quoted in The Silence of Unknowing by Terence Grant)

Week One

"I Am the Light of the World"

Then Jesus spoke to them again, saying, "I am the light of the world. He who follows Me shall not walk in darkness, but have the light of life." (John 8:12)

How Great Thou Art

English words by Stuart K. Hine (1899-1989)

This hymn has a weaving path through different languages and human experiences ending in the hymn we sing today. Carl Boberg, of Sweden wrote a nine stanza poem after a sudden thunder, lightening and rain storm. When he saw the rainbow, heard the birds singing, and saw the bright sunlight after such a violent storm, he wrote a poem in awe of God. The poem was sung to an old Swedish folk tune. The hymn was then translated into German (1907), into Russian (1912), then the nine verses into English by E. Gustav Johnson (1925). However, the song we sing today is a version re-written by Stuart K. Hine (1949) that became an international favorite due to the Billy Graham's Evangelistic Team.

As a young person, Hine was greatly influenced by Charles Spurgeon. While on a missionary trip to the Ukraine, Hine first heard the hymn in Russian and began to re-write the lyrics and create new ones. Hines added verse three based on this experience:

> It was typical of the Hines to ask if there were any Christians in the villages they visited. In one case, they found out that the only Christians that their host knew about were a man named Dmitri and his wife Lyudmila. Dmitri's wife knew how to read – evidently a fairly rare thing at that time and in that place. She taught herself how to read because a Russian soldier had left a Bible behind several years earlier, and she started slowly learning by reading that Bible. When the Hines arrived in the village and approached Dmitri's house, they heard a strange and wonderful sound: Dmitri's wife was reading from the gospel of John about the crucifixion of Christ to a houseful of guests, and those visitors were in the very act of repenting. In Ukraine (as I know firsthand!), this act of repenting is done very much out loud. So the Hines heard people calling out to God, saying how unbelievable it was that Christ would die for their own sins, and praising Him for His love and mercy. They just couldn't barge in and disrupt this obvious work of the Holy Spirit, so they stayed outside and listened. Stuart wrote down the phrases he heard the Repenters use, and (even though this was all in Russian), it became the third verse that we know today: "And when I think that God, His Son not sparing, Sent Him to die, I scarce can take it in."

While ministering to the exiled Polish community who desired to return home after WWII, one of the professing refugee Christians expressed his anticipation of the second coming of Christ that became Hine's inspiration for the 4th verse.

One man to whom they were ministering told them an amazing story: he had been separated from his wife at the very end of the war, and had not seen her since. At the time they were separated, his wife was a Christian, but he was not, but he had since been converted. His deep desire was to find his wife so they could at last share their faith together. But he told the Hines that he did not think he would ever see his wife on earth again. Instead he was longing for the day when they would meet in heaven, and could share in the Life Eternal there. These words again inspired Hine, and they became the basis for his fourth and final verse to 'How Great Thou Art': "When Christ shall come with shout of acclamation to take me home, what joy shall fill my heart. Then we shall bow in humble adoration and there proclaim, My God How Great Thou Art!"

How Great Thou Art
Stuart K. Hine

O Lord my God! When I in awesome wonder
Consider all the works Thy hand hath made.
I see the stars, I hear the rolling thunder,
Thy power throughout the universe displayed.

Refrain:
Then sings my soul, my Saviour God, to Thee;
How great Thou art, how great Thou art!
Then sings my soul, my Saviour God, to Thee:
How great Thou art, how great Thou art!

When through the woods and forest glades I wander
And hear the birds sing sweetly in the trees;
When I look down from lofty mountain grandeur
And hear the brook and feel the gentle breeze:
(Repeat Refrain.)

And when I think that God, His Son not sparing,
Sent Him to die, I scarce can take it in;
That on the cross, my burden gladly bearing,
He bled and died to take away my sin:
(Repeat Refrain.)

When Christ shall come with shout of acclamation
And take me home, what joy shall fill my heart!
Then I shall bow in humble adoration,
And there proclaim, my God, how great Thou art!

Jesus is the Light of the World

I was regretting the past and fearing the future. Suddenly, my Lord was speaking: **"My Name is I am"**. *When you live in the past with its mistakes and regrets, it is hard. I am not there. My name is not* **I Was.** *When you live in the future, with its problems and fears, it is hard. I am not there. My name is not* **I Will Be.** *When you live in this moment, it is not hard. I am here.* **My name is I am!**

~Helen Mallicoat (source quoted in The Silence of Unknowing by Terence Grant)

The Gospel of John is uniquely built around the seven "I Am" statements of Jesus. Most of these revelations of who He is are linked to a miracle that brings further revelation of that truth through the manifestation of the Spirit.

This week you will begin to study the first revelation of Jesus being the 'Light of the World' in John chapter 8. You will see many amazing things in Jesus' interactions with the woman caught in the act of adultery.

Jesus was always on mission to reveal His Father. He came to earth in the form of a man to reveal to us the loving ways of His Father. Jesus uses the same "I Am "statement in John 9 as He interacts with a blind man. (Read John 9:1-11) The focus of your study will be on the primary passage of John 8.

God desires for His works to be revealed in us too. One way we reveal Jesus to a dark world is to walk in the light each day. **A saint is someone who the light shines through to others.**

Days One and Two:

*Please note that the first week of homework is foundational to our entire seven weeks of study. This week's homework is a little longer than the subsequent six weeks. This week will be a crucial building block in our understanding the words of Jesus.

We start with the 'light of the world' because this was the first aspect of God's creation: Then God said, "Let there be light", and there was light. (Genesis 1:3)

Read John 8: 1-12

1. Record the facts of this interaction between the woman, the Pharisees and Jesus in bullet point form:

2. Verse 9 is the critical turning point in this story. Tell in your own words, what happens to the very ones who brought the accused woman to Jesus:

3. What 2 things does Jesus say to the woman and what does this reveal about how He views her sin?

4. Look up the following Scriptures and write out things you learn about Pharisees and teachers of the Law:

Mark 7:3:

Matt. 23:3:

Matt. 23:29-30; 31-33:

Luke 18:11-12:

Luke 16:15:

5. Look up Leviticus 20:10 and tell about the Law and the consequences for violating it.

6. How did Jesus respond to the Pharisees entrance onto the scene and their questioning of Him? Do you find His response odd? Why or why not?

7. Write out the things Jesus said in John 8:12. How do His words impact your life today?

Day Three

Jesus told the crowd observing Him in the temple as He interacted with the woman caught in adultery in John 8:12, that anyone who follows Him will no longer walk in darkness, but will have the 'light of life'. Through His light, we gain wisdom and spiritual insight for living.

1. Read Proverbs 8:22-32. Go verse-by-verse and list one aspect from each verse that speaks to you in a fresh way about the 'Wisdom of God'-- Jesus, the Word, the Living Logos, existing before time began:
v.22-Wisdom was brought forth at the beginning of 'His way'

v.23-

v.24-

v.25-

v.26-

v.27-

v.28-

v.29-

v.30-

v.31-

v.32-

2. Read Colossians 1:15-20, then write out in bullet points the truths of Who Jesus really is based on this passage of Scripture.

.

3.   Now take your bullet points based on the Colossians passage, and paraphrase them into language that a non-Christian could begin to relate to and understand. Be mindful of explaining Who Jesus is based on your audience.

**Challenge: Pray for a specific opportunity in the next week to share Who Jesus is!

4. Read John 1:4 out of several translations if they are available to you. Write out the verse in your favorite translation here:

5. What are the two outstanding dynamics that are found in Christ based on this verse? How are these two dynamics a reality in your life today? Be very specific.

6. Look up the following Scriptures and write out what you think the main point Jesus is making by these statements:
- Matthew 5:14-16

- Matthew 6:22-23

- Luke 8:16-18

- Luke 15:8-10

- John 5:35-39

7. Read John 1:9 again along with Isaiah 49:6. What do you think these 2 verses mean, taken together? (Who is a Gentile?)

8. In light of the verses you summarized above, now read and summarize the following passage: Hebrews 1: 1-4. Make sure you include the seven 'excellencies' of God's Son.

What does it mean to you to walk and live in the light?

Day Four:

Before the woman 'caught in the act of adultery' encountered Jesus, she encountered the Pharisees and the teachers of the law. These religious leaders were the personification of the law, while Jesus is Grace personified.

Take some time today to read through the various definitions and statements provided here to see the contrast between law and grace.

Grace- Charis- Strong's #5485- Divine favor and blessing; that brings joy, pleasure, delight, loveliness, grace of speech, good will, loving-kindness. Grace is the divine influence upon the heart and its reflection in life.

Before we can fully appreciate grace and all that means for us, we need to take a look at the Law and how it figures into our particular story as well as the story of our own lives. As you study today, ask the Lord to teach you through His Word and to make you even more aware of His wonderful gift of salvation to you by grace, through faith.

1. What is the purpose of the Law according to Romans 7:7?

2. What does the scripture say is the condition of those under the law in Galatians 3:10?

3. In Galatians 3:19, we are taught that the law was _____ because of _____ (sin).

4. It's been said that at first sin is **pleasing; then it becomes easy, then delightful, then frequent, and then it is a full-blown habit.**

Read Romans 6:23. What is the <u>wage</u> of sin?

• A <u>wage</u> was a ration or stipend originally given to a soldier in military service. Today, a wage is something that is owed to us; payment for work done; recompense.

• Read John 8:34. Summarize from your brief study of these verses and word meanings what sin does to us.

5. Read Galatians 5:16-17, 19-21. What is at war with our walk in the Spirit? List out the works of the flesh:

Day 5

Jesus told the woman caught in the act of adultery that He did not condemn her.

1.   Read Romans 8:1-5 and answer the following questions:

• What should a Christian do if she is experiencing condemnation?

• How are we to walk?

• What has the law of the Spirit done for you?

• What did God do for you?

• How is the righteous requirement of the law met in you?

• How do you practically set your mind on things of the spirit?

2.   Read and write out John 3:17-18.

 • Why did Jesus come according to this passage?

 • Do you think His purpose was revealed in His interaction with the woman in John 8?

 • Spend some time today in worship, praise and thanks for all Jesus has done for you! Sing the hymn, "How Great Thou Art," provided in this chapter.

"It's Christmas that dawns on you, and you only really believe in Christmas when you really live it. When you light a dark world and the unexpected places with a brave flame of joy; when you warm the cold, hopeless places with the daring joy that God is with us, God is for us, God is in us; when you are a wick to light hope in the dark—then you believe in Christmas. When you really believe in Christmas, you believe there is really hope for everyone. When you get Christmas, people get hope from you—don't lose it." ~Ann Voskamp

Week Two

"I Am the Bread of Life"

And Jesus said to them, "I am the bread of life. He who comes to Me shall never hunger, and he who believes in Me shall never thirst."
(John 6:35)

My Jesus, I love Thee

William R. Featherston (1846-1873)

It's thought that this poem of gratitude was written by 16-year-old William Featherston of Montreal, Canada, at the time of his conversion. It is believed that he mailed it to his aunt in Los Angeles. Somehow, the text ended up in The London Book, in 1864. Many years later, the founder of Gordon College and Gordon-Conwell Theological Seminary, the Rev. A. J. Gordon, wrote a melody for the poem. This hymn is found in nearly every evangelical hymnal and is frequently sung by saints as a renewed devotion to their sovereign Lord.

My Jesus I love Thee
William R. Featherston

Lord Jesus, I love Thee, I know Thou art mine;
For Thee all the pleasures of sin I resign;
My gracious Redeemer, my Savior art Thou,
If ever I loved Thee, Lord Jesus, 'tis now.
I love Thee, because Thou hast first loved me,
And purchased my pardon on Calvary's tree;
I love Thee for wearing the thorns on Thy brow;
If ever I loved Thee, Lord Jesus, 'tis now.
I'll love Thee in life, I will love Thee in death,
And praise Thee as long as Thou lendest me breath;
And say when the death-dew lies cold on my brow,
If ever I loved Thee, Lord Jesus, 'tis now.
In mansions of glory and endless delight
I'll ever adore Thee in glory so bright;
I'll sing with the glittering crown on my brow,
If ever I loved Thee, Lord Jesus, 'tis now. Jesus is the Bread of Life

Day One:

Give yourself adequate time to read the story of Jesus, His disciples, the multitudes, and the miracle as He makes His first "I Am" statement in John 6: 1-59

1. In verses 5-9, what are your observations as to the disciples' concerns? What was their focus?

2. What insight do you glean from verse 6?

3. What does Jesus do in verses 10-15? Summarize your conclusions.

4. What did Jesus say was the reason why the people sought Him according to verse 26? What do you think is the 'food that spoils' that Jesus spoke of in verse 27? What did Jesus say is the one work we are to do, according to verse 29?

Day Two:

Read John 6: 22-40

1. What are the questions the people asked of Jesus in verses 25, 28, and 30?

2. What do their questions reveal about where they placed their emphasis and hope?

3. How did Jesus respond to the questions of the people? List out His responses from verses 26, 27, 29, 32-33.

4. In John 6:29, Jesus tells us the main work we are to do. What is that work, and expound on that by reading I John 3:23 and listing the truth from this verse.

5. Once the people hear that Jesus will give them true bread from heaven, the people ask for this bread (v. 34). What truth does Jesus reveal in verses 35-40?

Day Three:

Read John 6:35-40

A key word in John's Gospel is 'believe'. Our faith is so important to our understanding of Scripture. We are to know Jesus in spirit and in truth. To walk in faith, we must know the truth of who Jesus is and to experience, by the Spirit, the reality of that truth.

It is vital that our faith be more than just head knowledge. Our hearts must be affected by the truth of who Jesus is. Jesus made it a point to reveal who He is by giving the 7 'I am' statements.

When He told the people He is the Bread of Life, He was revealing that He is the true, life-sustaining power that we all need—there is no substitute for Him.

1. Look up verses 35, 48, and 51 in John 6. Write out the three things Jesus said about Himself.

2. Why do you think it is significant that Jesus revealed this 3 times?

3. In the passage from today, write out the truth from each verse that Jesus revealed to the people:

- V. 35-

- V. 36-

- V 37-

- V. 38-

- V. 39-

- V. 40-

4. From your three-day study of the 'Bread of Life' so far, write out a prayer, thanking Jesus for all that He is to you, listing the specific truths you have gleaned from this passage

Day Four:

When Jesus revealed Himself as the 'Bread of Life', there was an unmistakable parallel to God's covenant Name that He revealed to Moses in Exodus 3:14.

1. Read Exodus 3:14 and write out the name God revealed to Moses.

Revealing His divine named declares His character and attributes, showing that the issue is not who Moses is, but who is with him. This name is related to the Hebrew verb meaning 'to be', and it shows the absolute existence of God. The Hebrew here is also the source of our English name for God, "Yahweh", "Jehovah', or "Lord".

2. For the greater context of the background, history and story (His story) of Jesus revealing His name as the 'Bread of Life', read all of Exodus 16. Reading this chapter is so critical to understanding this aspect of who Jesus is. Pease take the time to read this today. Write down in the space provided, insights or questions you have from this passage:

Day Five:

Psalm 78 is another important passage in our understanding of Jesus being the 'Bread of Life'. This psalm tells the story of God's kindness to Israel despite their rebellion of Him in the desert. We can be comforted, knowing that even when we fail, God understands our weaknesses and forgives us when we ask of Him.

This psalm also reveals the importance of passing along our faith to the generations coming behind us.

Read through all of Psalm 78 and answer the following questions:
- How did God prove/show His kindness to Israel over the years?

- How did Israel respond to His kindness?

- What kinds of emotion are displayed by God and revealed by this Psalm?

- What are some attributes displayed by God throughout this Psalm? (list the verses)

• What did God desire from the Israelites?

• In v. 41 the Psalm says, "Again and again, they tempted God and limited the Holy One of Israel." How can mere humans 'limit' God? What does this verse mean?

Week Three

"I Am the Door"

"I am the door. If anyone enters by Me, he will be saved, and will go in and out and find pasture." (John 10:9)

I Surrender All

Judson W. Van de Venter (1855-1939)

Judson Van de Venter was an American art teacher and musician. He struggled with putting down his artwork and teaching to move into full time evangelical ministry. It took five years of wrestling to leave his teaching job. The foundation of this hymn in his own words:

For some time, I had struggled between developing my talents in the field of art and going into full- time evangelistic work. At last the pivotal hour of my life came, and I surrendered all. A new day was ushered into my life. I became an evangelist and discovered down deep in my soul a talent hitherto unknown to me. God had hidden a song in my heart, and touching a tender chord, He caused me to sing.

Toward the end of Judson's life, he taught at the Florida Bible Institute in the 1920s. After retirement, he continued to invest and influence students with his music. The Rev. Billy Graham attended the Institute in the 1930s and was heavily impacted by Judson's hymns, specifically "I Surrender All" as Graham popularized this hymn through his crusades and revivals in the 1940s. Like Judson, you never know whom you will influence through your obedience.

Michael Hawn wrote some interesting insights of the hymn worth noting:

> In keeping with the gospel tradition, "I Surrender All" repeats key words throughout the hymn. Each stanza begins with "All to Jesus I surrender". The hymn's chorus repeats "I surrender all" three times, and an additional two times in the men's part. The entire hymn, if sung with each refrain and second-voice part, contains the word "surrender" 30 times, and the word "all" 43 times.
>
> The hymn's first stanza stresses complete surrender: "All to him I freely give". The second stanza surrenders worldly pleasures, and the third prays to "feel the Holy Spirit". Stanza four asks to be filled with Jesus's love, power, and blessing. In the fifth stanza, the singer feels "the sacred flame" – an image of the Holy Spirit – and the joy of "full salvation" born of surrender.

I Surrender All

Judson W. Van de Venter

All to Jesus I surrender;
all to him I freely give;
I will ever love and trust him,
in his presence daily live.

Refrain:
I surrender all,
I surrender all,
all to thee, my blessed Savior,
I surrender all.

All to Jesus I surrender;
humbly at his feet I bow,
worldly pleasures all forsaken;
take me, Jesus, take me now.
(Refrain)

All to Jesus I surrender;
make me, Savior, wholly thine;
fill me with thy love and power;
truly know that thou art mine.
(Refrain)

All to Jesus I surrender;
Lord, I give myself to thee;
fill me with thy love and power;
let thy blessing fall on me. (Refrain)

All to Jesus I surrender;
now I feel the sacred flame.
O the joy of full salvation!
Glory, glory, to his name!
(Refrain)

Jesus is the Door

When Jesus told his listeners and disciples that He is the door, it was at the end of a very long conversation with a bunch of Pharisees. Most of the time, having the greater context of a story or a conversation is very helpful to our overall understanding.

Understanding the Bible is critical to our faith journey. We will take the time in the first day of this study to glean the greater context before we begin to study Jesus' next 'I am' statement.

Day One:

1. Read all of John chapter 9 and answer the following questions:
    - What was the basic problem of the Pharisees?

    - Why do you think that the Pharisees did not think Jesus was from God? Give specifics.

    - How did the former blind man's parents respond to the religious leaders?

    - Why did the Pharisees ultimately cast the former blind man out of the temple/community?

2. Explain the spiritual significance of true vision and true blindness.

3. What personal applications do you glean from this study of chapter 9?

4. Spend some time as you wrap up your study, worshiping Jesus like the former blind man did in verse 38 of John 9. Maybe you want to write out your worship in a prayer journal. Maybe you want to put on your favorite praise music and sing at the top of your lungs to Him! Maybe you want to declare how good He is by saying Biblical truths out loud. Whichever method you choose, spend at a minimum, 5 minutes of total worship---include in your worship this phrase: "Lord, I believe!"

Day Two:

Read John 10:1-10

1. In verse 1, Jesus explains that some 'climb up other ways'. Explain various ways that we and others try to get to God. Are some of these ways contrary to Scripture? Why do we try to get to God by other means? Are you currently given to something that is a false way in your life?

2. Jesus says in verse 2 that he who enters by the door is the shepherd of the sheep. Look up the following Scriptures and write out what you learn further about the shepherd:

- Ephesians 4:11-

- John 10:11, 14, 16-

- Hebrews 13:20-

- 1 Peter 2:25-

3. Spend some time today prayerfully considering the work of a doorkeeper. What does it mean to be a doorkeeper of your own life? What are the doors of an individual person? In what ways can others, influences, opinions, evils, etc—enter the doorways of our lives? Do you think there is spiritual significance in 'shutting doors' in the spiritual realm? Why or why not?

4. List out the positive and proactive ways that you keep watch over the door of your heart and life. Prayerfully commit these to your Good Shepherd for safe-keeping.

Day Three:

Read John 10:1-10 again.
1. In verses 3 and 4, write out all the action steps of the 'players' involved and bullet point them.

2. What are some practical ways that you as a sheep, can hear the voice of the Shepherd?

3. What does it mean to you personally that Jesus calls you by your name?

4. If you were taking a new believer or even an unbeliever through this passage of Scripture, how would you explain to her that the sheep follow because they know his voice? What does that mean practically? How does this impact daily life? What are ways to cultivate knowing the voice of the shepherd?

Day Four:

1. Read John 10:1-10. In verses 5 & 6, Jesus explains that the sheep will not follow a stranger. What do you think He means by the term 'stranger'?

2. Look up 2 Corinthians 11:13-15. Who are the 'strangers'?

3. Why do you think that in verse 6, the religious leaders did not understand the things Jesus spoke to them?

4. Do you know anyone in your life currently that is following the voice of a stranger? How are you praying for them? How are you relating to them?

Day Five:

1. Summarize all of the words of Jesus in John 10: 7-10.

2. Read John 14:6 and Ephesians 2:18. Discuss how these 2 verses relate to our study of sheep, shepherds and doors.

3. Spend the rest of your study today reading through and meditating on Psalm 23. Read it in several translations.
   What are the benefits of following the Lord, according to this psalm?

4. What are the rod and staff? How are these significant to a shepherd?

5. What does verse 5 mean both practically and figuratively?

6. How does the promise of verse 6 bless you?

For Additional Study:

1. Spend some time reading the story of Achan and Joshua in Joshua 7. Record the facts out of that chapter.

2. What were the things/directives the Lord gave/said to Joshua?

3. How did Joshua appeal to Achan? How did Achan respond?

4. What do you think of all of this?

5. Now go and read the verse in Hosea 2:15, which references the Valley of Achor. Relate this scripture and the promise of God back to the story in Joshua. What lessons/applications are meaningful to you and why?

6. Finish your study by spending 2 or 3 days in Psalm 71.
How does this psalm encourage you personally? Is there a verse out of this psalm that you can commit to memory that is especially meaningful to you?

Week Four

"I Am the Good Shepherd"

"I am the good shepherd. The good shepherd gives His life for the sheep."
(John 10:11)

He Leadeth Me

Joseph H. Gilmore (1834-1918)

Twenty-eight-year-old Pastor Gilmore was preaching on Psalm 23, a sermon he had given a few times before as a pastoral student, when he just couldn't get past the phrase, "He leadeth me." So he made that phrase the theme of his sermon. After the service, while sitting with friends, discussing the blessing of divine guidance, he took a page from his sermon notes, wrote the entire hymn from start to finish on the back. Then handed the page to his wife and never thought a thing about it again.

His wife submitted the hymn to The Watchman and Reflector. She felt the words would bless fellow countrymen during the dark days of the Civil War. Joseph recounted how he found out what his wife had done.

> I did not know until 1865 that my hymn had been set to music by William B. Bradbury. I went to Rochester to preach as a candidate before the Second Baptist Church. Going into the chapel on arrival in the city, I picked up a hymnal to see what they were singing and opened it at my own hymn, "He Leadeth Me."

William Bradbury, the famous hymn composer had seen the hymn, added music and the last two lines of the chorus.

He Leadeth Me
Joseph H. Gilmore

He leadeth me, O blessèd thought!
O words with heav'nly comfort fraught!
Whate'er I do, where'er I be
Still 'tis God's hand that leadeth me.

Refrain

He leadeth me, He leadeth me,
By His own hand He leadeth me;
His faithful follower I would be,
For by His hand He leadeth me.

Sometimes mid scenes of deepest gloom,
Sometimes where Eden's bowers bloom,
By waters still, o'er troubled sea,
Still 'tis His hand that leadeth me.

Refrain

Lord, I would place my hand in Thine,
Nor ever murmur nor repine;
Content, whatever lot I see,
Since 'tis my God that leadeth me.

Refrain

And when my task on earth is done,
When by Thy grace the vict'ry's won,
E'en death's cold wave I will not flee,
Since God through Jordan leadeth me.

Refrain

Jesus is the Good Shepherd

When my children were little, one of our favorite books to read was Sheep in a Jeep. Even though we read it at least one hundred times, it never ceased to entertain me and make me chuckle because it depicted the helplessness of sheep. Sheep are totally dependent creatures. They are prone to wander, and when they do escape, many times they are unable to find their way back to the sheepfold. The helplessness of sheep explains why a good shepherd, who in the Bible, is a case study in care and compassion, is so important.

Day One:

Read John 10:1-15 for the entire context of Jesus' 4th "I am" statement.

1. Make a list highlighting the following:
   * Characteristics of sheep:

   * Characteristics of a shepherd:

   * The benefit of a sheepfold:

   * The benefit of a doorkeeper:

2. Jesus is speaking figuratively here, communicating profound truth by using an everyday economic industry example in ancient Palestine. Please answer the following:

   * What is the truth Jesus wants His listeners to glean from the analogy of shepherds and sheep?

- Where do you see yourself in the analogy?

- What do you learn personally from it?

- Do you currently serve as a 'shepherd' in someone's spiritual walk? Does someone 'shepherd' you?

3. Look up the following verses and describe the Messiah's responsibility as one of feeding and shepherding:

- Isaiah 40:11-

- Psalm 80:1-

- Ezekiel 34:23-

- Micah 5:4-

Which verse really spoke to you and why?

Close out your study time today by praising God for His leadership and shepherding of you. Vocalize specific praise to your Good Shepherd. Choose your favorite hymn from the study and sing them in praise to your Good Shepherd.

41

Day Two:

Read Psalm 23.
This pastoral psalm reflects absolute trust and a peaceful confidence in God.

1. In the first 4 verses, David speaks of God as his personal shepherd. List out the ways that David expresses his trust of God's provision. Next to each provision you list, suggest a current way the Lord provides for us today in our world. Example: green pastures—I have a peaceful, comforting home.

2. The picture of God as the Shepherd is totally fulfilled and completed (perfectly perfect!) in Jesus Christ, the Good Shepherd in John 10. Look up Hebrews 13:20 and 1 Peter 5:4 and give two other shepherd names listed for Jesus.

3. In verse 3, David declares that the Lord restores his soul. What do you think he means by this? How do you think God accomplishes this? Read 2 Corinthians 4: 16-18 to help you answer.

Day Three:

Read Psalm 23 again today out loud and as a prayer and declaration of your faith before God, praising Him for all of His provisions in your life.

1. David says in verse 4 that God being with him is all that matters. God's on-going Presence in his life is the key to his trust. The Lord had this identical message to another faithful servant in Joshua 1:5-9. Read the conversation and list out in bullet points, everything the Lord promised Joshua:

2. How important is the Bible in light of enjoying God's daily on-going Presence? If you were trying to convince someone of this necessity, what would you tell them?

3. Spend some time today recording in your journal, all the ways you have sensed God's Presence this week. Thank Him for each instance. Ask Him to increase your sensitivity in this area. Sing through a couple of the hymns, including, "He Leadeth Me".

Day Four:

Today we will be spending our study time in Ezekiel chapter 34. Take the time to read the entire 31 verses.

1. This chapter is divided into 2 parts:

   1) The irresponsible shepherds vs. 1-10
   2) God, the true shepherd vs. 11-31

Make a contrast list (it's a helpful learning tool to contrast principles) of each category.

The irresponsible: The True:

2. How has this exercise strengthened your faith in God, the true Shepherd, and Jesus, the Good Shepherd—the completion of that? What did you see? What did you learn? Who had the longer list? Summarize your insights to share with your group:

Day Five

1. Read the parable of the lost sheep in Matthew 18: 10-14. What new thing, if any, do you learn about the Good Shepherd and the sheep? How does this strengthen your faith?

2. A word about worry.....look up the following scriptures and record what you learn about anxiety vs. trust:
- Philippians 4: 6 & 13 & 19-

- Matthew 6:25-

- 1 Peter 5:7-

- 1 Thessalonians 5:17, 18-

- John 15:5-

- Psalm 23:1-

- 2 Corinthians 9:8-

Take your findings and re-write them into a prayer for your own life and those you love.

Further Study:
1. This week marks the half-way point of our study through the 'I am'. Go back through the previous studies and teaching notes and begin to create a list of the I Am statements of Jesus. Under each name, write out the specific aspects of how He fulfills that name with things you've gleaned.

2. If you are interested in how David's life turned out or how the Lord was with Joshua, use a concordance to find the references that will enable you to read more about these 2 men. Find out how the Lord used them for His purposes and how the Lord was with each one.

3. What did you learn from your biographical study?

4. Write out a short, current testimony of your own life and how the Lord's Presence has guided you most recently. Which 'I Am" statement of Jesus would you use to describe His activity in your life in recent months?

Week Five

"I Am the Resurrection and the Life"

Jesus said to her, "I am the resurrection and the life. He who believes in Me, though he may die, he shall live." (John 11: 25-26)

It Is Well With My Soul
Horatio G. Spafford (1828 – 1888)

Horatio, faithful husband and father, a successful attorney, active Presbyterian Church member, good friend and supporter of D.L. Moody had a very happy life when tragedy suddenly struck.
He saw his investments go up in flames, literally, in the Chicago fire. He lost it all in one night. Right before the fire, his son had died.

Horatio decided to take his family to Europe as a break from their personal hardship and to support Moody's evangelistic efforts in the U.K. Due to a business issue; Horatio sent his wife and four daughters on ahead, planning to join them shortly.

> "On November 22 the ship was struck by the Lochearn, an English vessel, and sank in twelve minutes. Several days later the survivors were finally landed at Cardiff, Wales, and Mrs. Spafford cabled her husband, 'Saved alone.'"

Spafford left immediately to join his wife. This hymn is said to have been penned as he approached the area of the ocean thought to be where the ship carrying his daughters had sunk.

Horatio and his wife did have more children. They moved to Jerusalem, partnered with Swedish Christians to establish the American Colony, solely a philanthropic effort regardless of religious affiliation with Muslims, Jews and Christians to gain trust and build community not to proselytize. The American Colony was instrumental in providing food, orphanages and medical supplies during and after WWI for the community. Novelist Selma Lagerlof used the American Colony as the subject in her Noble prize winning Jerusalem.

It Is Well With My Soul
Horatio G. Spafford

When peace, like a river, attendeth my way,
When sorrows like sea billows roll;
Whatever my lot, Thou hast taught me to say,
It is well, it is well with my soul.

Refrain:
It is well with my soul,
It is well, it is well with my soul.
It is well, it is well with my soul.

Though Satan should buffet, though trials should come,
Let this blest assurance control,
That Christ hath regarded my helpless estate,
And hath shed His own blood for my soul.

My sin—oh, the bliss of this glorious thought!—
My sin, not in part but the whole,
Is nailed to the cross, and I bear it no more,
Praise the Lord, praise the Lord, O my soul!

For me, be it Christ, be it Christ hence to live:
If Jordan above me shall roll,
No pang shall be mine, for in death as in life
Thou wilt whisper Thy peace to my soul.

But, Lord, 'tis for Thee, for Thy coming we wait,
The sky, not the grave, is our goal;
Oh, trump of the angel! Oh, voice of the Lord!
Blessed hope, blessed rest of my soul!

And Lord, haste the day when the faith shall be sight,
The clouds be rolled back as a scroll;
The trump shall resound, and the Lord shall descend,
Even so, it is well with my soul.

Jesus is the Resurrection and the Life

Day One:

Read John 11: 1-46

1. Write down anything you see from the text that jumps out at you in a meaningful way. Take some notes in the space provided for you:

2. How were you impacted by the inclusion of 'a certain man, Lazarus of Bethany, the town of Mary and her sister Martha'? How do you feel about being known so intimately by the Savior? How does this impact you? Your interactions with others? Your family relationships?

3. Read another story about Mary and Martha in Luke 10:38-42. What new things do you see from this interaction with Jesus that confirms what you learned about their friendship from our lesson?

Day Two:

1. Today you will spend the entire session on Mary's act of 'extravagant worship'. In Matthew 26:6-13, read the story for yourself and record all of the events as they unfolded. (Where was Jesus as this story took place?)

2. What do you think of the disciples' reaction to Mary's act of worship? How do you think you would have reacted if you had been there? The approximate worth of the perfume is $46,000 in today's currency. Can you understand, in light of the large amount of money 'poured out' on Jesus, their reaction?

3. Read the same story in another gospel: John 12:1-8. What new information do you glean from this story? Do you see the dynamics of friendship and acceptance in this setting of Bethany? What do you think of Jesus' defense of Mary in v. 7?

4. What practical things do you learn about worship from this brief study—both personally and corporately? Is there anything in your life that God has 'nudged' you about regarding your own acts of worship?

Day Three:

1. Today we return to our text in John 11: 1-27. In verse 3, we see that the sisters sent Jesus a message. We send 'messages' to Jesus today too through our prayer lives. Look up Isaiah 43:26 in several translations if possible. How does this verse minister to you in light of your personal prayer times?

2. In verse 4, Jesus said that what was happening to Lazarus would be for God's glory. We can define God's glory in part as: completing an assignment and displaying the splendor of God Himself to a watching world. What do you think God's glory means for the following:

•   For the sisters:

•   For Lazarus:

•   For the disciples:

3. What do you think of the actions of Jesus in light of the fact that He loves these 3 siblings? How does the truth of John 6:29 come into play in this story?

Days Four & Five:

1. Read John 11:9-14 again. Summarize what you believe Jesus is communicating from these verses.

2. In John 11:17-27, the conversation with Jesus and Martha takes a drastic turn and Martha makes an amazing faith declaration. Explain how our words of faith impact our daily lives. Take some time to write down 5 personal faith declarations from your lesson this week.

3. Jesus doesn't care so much about what we know; He cares about what we believe! Write out John 6:29 again here:

4. Review the faith declarations included in the book and say a few out loud each day.

Week Six

"I Am the Way, the Truth, and the Life"

Jesus said to him, "
I am the way, the truth,
and the life.
No one comes to the Father
except through Me."
(John 14:6)

Trust and Obey

By John H. Sammis, 1887

John Sammis was called by God to leave his business career and attend seminary. He was ordained as a Presbyterian pastor in 1880, served at several churches, then joined the faculty of the Los Angeles Bible Institute.

The hymn was inspired in 1886 when the composer of the music, Daniel B. Towner (1850-1919), was the music leader during one of Dwight L. Moody's famous revivals. Towner provided the following account cited by Moody's musical partner, Ira D. Sankey, in his biography, My Life and the Story of the Gospel Hymns:

"Mr. Moody was conducting a series of meetings in Brockton, Massachusetts, and I had the pleasure of singing for him there. One night a young man rose in a testimony meeting and said, 'I am not quite sure—but I am going to trust, and I am going to obey.' I just jotted that sentence down, and sent it with a little story to the Rev. J. H. Sammis, a Presbyterian minister. He wrote the hymn, and the tune was born."

Trust and Obey
John H. Sammis

When we walk with the Lord in the light of His Word,
What a glory He sheds on our way!
While we do His good will, He abides with us still,
And with all who will trust and obey.

Refrain:
Trust and obey, for there's no other way
To be happy in Jesus, but to trust and obey.

Not a shadow can rise, not a cloud in the skies,
But His smile quickly drives it away;
Not a doubt or a fear, not a sigh or a tear,
Can abide while we trust and obey.

Not a burden we bear, not a sorrow we share,
But our toil He doth richly repay;
Not a grief or a loss, not a frown or a cross,
But is blessed if we trust and obey.

But we never can prove the delights of His love
Until all on the altar we lay;
For the favor He shows, for the joy
He bestows, Are for them who will trust and obey.

Then in fellowship sweet we will sit at His feet,
Or we'll walk by His side in the way;
What He says we will do, where He sends we will go;
Never fear, only trust and obey.

Jesus is the Way, the Truth, and the Life

Day One:
Read John 14:1-6—Jesus is the map, the road, and the destination!

1. Most of these verses are the words of Jesus. What especially encourages you out of these verses and why?

2. How is it possible to not 'let' our hearts be troubled? What does this mean for you personally? What are some practical ways that you can cultivate an 'untroubled' heart?

3. Jesus said to His followers in John 14:27 that He would leave something with them. What is it? How is it different than what the world offers? What command does He repeat again in this verse? What does He add to this command that is different from verse 1?

4. Take your 'gleanings' from your study time today and write out a prayer to your Lord, committing afresh to not 'let your heart' be troubled.

Day Two:

1. Read John 14: 7-11. We have said throughout our study, that Jesus was always pointing us to His Father. Why did He do this? What is the significance of this? How have you grown in knowing the Father through this study so far? What has been revealed to you about the love of God that you had not seen before?

2. In verses 8-9, Jesus and Philip have a conversation. Do you think Jesus is a bit exasperated with Philip? Why or why not? What do you think Philip was looking for or hoping to see?

3. Jesus revealed that if anyone had seen Him (Jesus), they had seen the Father. What does this mean to you in the 21st century? How does Jesus show you the Father?

4. Read John 10:37-38 along with John 14: 10-11 and 20-21. What are the basics of what Jesus is revealing through all of these verses? How does obeying or keeping the commandments of Jesus further our relationship with Him?

5. The word **manifest** in verse 21 is **emphanidzo** in the Greek. (Sounds awfully similar to emphasize doesn't it?) It means to cause to shine; to appear; to come to view; to reveal to exhibit; to make visible; to be conspicuous. (Strong's #1718)

In verse 21, it is the self-revelation of Jesus to believers. Wow! How is this tied to our obedience as followers of Christ? How does this motivate you in your own walk of devotion to Him?

Day Three:

1. We have learned through this brief study that Jesus is the way to the Father; He is the truth about God and the very life of God. Look up the following Scripture passages and write out how these passages tie in to Jesus' 3-pronged I Am statement: "I am the way, the truth, and the life." How do these passages confirm what Jesus revealed?

- Hebrews 10: 19-20:

- John 1:14, 17:

- John 8:13-19; 32:

- John 10:7-10:

- John 18:28-38:

Days Four & Five:

1. Go back and read John 14:1-6 again in light of the further study you have done. How has your understanding of Jesus being the way, the truth, and the life expanded through your study? How would you explain this to an unbeliever who was genuinely searching for truth?

2. Read verse 6 along with I Timothy 2:5-6 and Galatians 3:19-20. Explain what it means to have a mediator in two ways: explain it to an unbeliever and then express what it means to you as a ransomed, redeemed, daughter of the King!

3. How does John 14:1 compare with Philippians 4:6-7? How can you connect the dots to what Jesus commanded and what Paul echoed in his letter to the church at Philippi?

4. Write out your own 'story' or testimony of how you have come to know and love Jesus as **the way, the truth and the life**. Make sure you 'emphasize' what your life has been like since Jesus took over as Lord. Oftentimes, Christians will emphasize or focus on what life was like before Jesus (all the good, bad, and the ugly!), but <u>the most important aspect</u> of telling your story is revealing Jesus to a dark and hurting world.

Week Seven

"I Am the True Vine"

*"I am the true vine, and
My Father is the vinedresser."
(John 15:1)*

I Need Thee Every Hour

Annie S. Hawks (1835-1918) Refrain added by Robert Lowry

Pastor Dr. Robert Lowry who wrote many gospel songs encouraged Annie to cultivate her gift of writing poetry that began when she was a young girl. Annie wrote over 400 hymns but this is the only one sung today. It was Lowry who wrote the refrain and the music.

Annie herself describes how the hymn came about.

> *"One day as a young wife and mother of 37 years of age, I was busy with my regular household tasks during a bright June morning [in 1872]. Suddenly, I became so filled with the sense of nearness to the Master that, wondering how one could live without Him, either in joy or pain, these words were ushered into my mind, the thought at once taking full possession of me – 'I Need Thee Every Hour...'"*

In reflection of the deep meaning of this hymn, years later when Annie's husband died she said,

> *"I did not understand at first why this hymn had touched the great throbbing heart of humanity. It was not until long after, when the shadow fell over my way, the shadow of a great loss, that I understood something of the comforting power in the words which I had been permitted to give out to others in my hour of sweet serenity and peace."*

This hymn of submission is foreign in today's culture. In the depths of our soul, we need Christ our Savior. When we are low, desperate, and heavily burdened He promises "all who labor and are heavy laden, and I will give you rest" (Matthew 11:28). Humble yourself before the Risen Savior, press into Him and rest in His full atonement of your sins.

I Need Thee Every Hour
Annie S. Hawks
Refrain added by Robert Lowry

I need Thee every hour, most gracious Lord;
No tender voice like Thine can peace afford.

Refrain:
I need Thee, oh, I need Thee;
Every hour I need Thee;
Oh, bless me now, my Savior,
I come to Thee.

I need Thee every hour, stay Thou nearby;
Temptations lose their pow'r when Thou art nigh.

I need Thee every hour, in joy or pain;
Come quickly and abide, or life is vain.

I need Thee every hour; teach me Thy will;
And Thy rich promises in me fulfill.

I need Thee every hour, most Holy One;
Oh, make me Thine indeed, Thou blessed Son.

Jesus is the True Vine

Day One:

Read John 15:1-8

1. This is Jesus' seventh and last self-proclaimed 'I Am' statement. He describes in this passage, the relationship between Himself and His disciples. The background for this is Isaiah 5:1-7. Look up this passage. Who you think is the 'beloved' and who is the 'vineyard'? What similarities do you see with the John passage?

2. What happens to the fruitless branch in verses 2 and 6?

3. Summarize in your words, the relationship Jesus is describing with His disciples:

Day Two:

Read John 15:1-8

1. In the space below, highlighting the True Vine; Vinedresser; Branches, under each column, write down from the passage:
    (1) What each 'character' does
    (2) Action taken towards them
    (3) Commands to follow
    (4) Benefits of obedience

<u>True Vine</u>   <u>Vinedresser</u>   <u>Branches</u>

2. What practical application did you receive from the exercise above? How will you implement what you are learning from the Scriptures?

Day Three:

I. Jesus used tangible objects of His day to teach profound principles of the Kingdom to His predominantly agrarian audience. We are going to try this same strategy! Use the space provided to free-hand draw a vine with branches. Illustrate your branches with some type of 'fruit' on them: either leafy, healthy flowers or leaves—or—fruits. After you've drawn your picture, write out on your design, what kind of fruit you want to see on your branches as a Christ-lover and follower.

2. Read Galatians 5:22-26. List out the fruits of the Spirit. Why do you think the Bible refers to these qualities as 'fruits'? How do these fruits and the way they are displayed in a life, relate to our story about the True Vine and the branches? Are we responsible for producing these fruits?

3. The nine 'fruits' of the Spirit can be broken down into 3 different categories. Try this on your own. How would you differentiate between the 3 categories?

70

Day Four:

1. Re-read John 15:5-8 today. Write out exactly what Jesus said in verse 7. What does it mean for 'His words to abide in us'? What does that look like in your life? Do you feel that His Words do indeed abide (take up permanent residence) in your life/heart/mind?

2. Read John 8:31-32. What are people called who abide in Jesus' word? What is a supreme benefit of abiding in His Word?

3. In John 15 in verses 4 and 5 Jesus says there is a definite result of not abiding in Him, what is that? Read 2 Corinthians 3:4-5. Where is our sufficiency from? How are we even able to abide?

4. Turn the results of your study today into a personal prayer, using specific Scripture as you pray.

Day Five:

His Word abiding in you:
Read: Hosea 14:1-9 (an OT example of a fruitful vine in restored Israel), choose one of the following Bible study methods to use for your study today:

- **Devotional Method:**
  *Pray for insight on how to apply the passage
  *Meditate on the verse or verses you have chosen to study
  *Write out an application
  *Memorize a key verse from your study

- **Chapter Analysis Method:**
  *Write out a chapter summary
  *List your observations
  *Ask questions
  *Correlate your chapter with other Scriptures
  *List some possible applications
  *Write down some concluding thoughts
  *Write out one application

- **Verse-by-verse Analysis Method:**
  *write out the verse/verses
  *write out the verse in your own personal paraphrase
  *ask questions about the verse that you have
  *find any cross-reference verses and look them up
  *write out your insights
  *write out your possible personal applications from your study

- **Word Study Method:**
  *Write out the word from the passage that speaks to you (example: abide)
  *write out the English definition from the dictionary
  *Look up different translations of the verse and compare the wording
  *Look up the Greek or Hebrew word or the root word if possible (Latin?)
  *write out any insights you have from your study

"The result of desire is often desired results."

"For as she thinks in her heart, so is she."
Proverbs 23: 7

Blessed Assurance

Frances J. Crosby

Blessed assurance, Jesus is mine!
Oh, what a foretaste of glory divine!
Heir of salvation, purchase of God,
Born of His Spirit, washed in His blood.

Refrain:
This is my story, this is my song,
Praising my Savior all the day long;
This is my story, this is my song,
Praising my Savior all the day long.

Perfect submission, perfect delight,
Visions of rapture now burst on my sight;
Angels, descending, bring from above
Echoes of mercy, whispers of love.

Perfect submission, all is at rest,
I in my Savior am happy and blest,
Watching and waiting, looking above,
Filled with His goodness, lost in His love.

What I Believe and Confess Based on the Word of God:
"I believe, therefore, I speak!" (2 Cor. 4:13)

• I abide in Christ and His words abide in me, therefore, I will ask what I will and it shall be done for me. I know that there is not an earthly father who ever desired to do more for his children than what my Heavenly Father desires to do for me. (John 15:7; Matt. 7:11)

• I will not worry about what I see or feel, or the presence of contradicting reports. God's Word is truth and will remain because it is eternal. I believe the truth of God's Word over the facts or circumstances. (John 1:1; 14-17)

• I walk in godliness and do not walk in the counsel of the ungodly, nor stand in the way of sinners, nor sit in the seat of the scornful, but my delight is in the law of the Lord. In God's Word I meditate day and night. Therefore, I am like a tree planted by the rivers of water. I bring forth fruit; my leaf does not wither and everything I do prospers." (Psalm 1: 1-3)

• "Put Me in remembrance" God has said to me. (Is. 43:26) I stand before the throne of grace and remind the Lord of His promises to me. I bring my case before Him and bring up His Word and promises. I come before God according to His Word and His Word does not fail. (Is. 55:11; 2Cor. 1:20; Heb. 4:16; 2Peter 1:3-4)

• I am more than a conqueror in all things through Christ who loves me. I face my life without fear because of this Bible truth. The law of the Spirit of life in Christ Jesus has made me free from the law of sin and death. (Rom. 8:2; 31-39)

• My God is able to make all grace abound towards me, that I always have all sufficiency in all things and bound in every good work. (2 Cor 9:8)

• For with God nothing is impossible. I possess the Spirit poured out on my life continually. I stand by my confession knowing that God cannot fail me. In the face of every need, I confess the Lord is my Shepherd, I shall not want. He is leading me and guiding me. If God is for me, who can be against me? Surely goodness and mercy shall follow me all the days of my life! (Ps. 23:1, 6; Matt. 19:26; Romans 5:5; 8:31)

• Greater is He that is in me than any force that can come against me in this world. He is my praise and He is my God who has done for me these great and awesome things which my eyes have seen. (Ps.146:1; 1 John 4:4)

Confessions for Children

- I am strong! The Lord is the strength of my life.
- With His stripes, I am healed. My body is healthy.
- God gives me the desires of my heart.
- I desire to have a focused brain. God is helping me and strengthening me.
- My brain is focused. I concentrate and get all my work done quickly. I am smart and my schoolwork is done correctly.
- I am creative. God is giving me lots of ideas for things He wants me to do.
- I have a destiny on my life. God has given me work to do that He has prepared for me beforehand.
- I am a leader. I am 'the head and not the tail.' I am an influencer for good.
- God is with me and He is my helper.
- My God supplies my every need.
- I am fully forgiven of all my sins.
- I do not fear because I trust in the Lord with all my heart, and I know that God has not given me a spirit of fear.
- I have no insecurity because I see myself the way God sees me.
- Jesus has made unto me wisdom. I am a thankful person.
- I love to tell others about Jesus.
- I love my family and my friends and my neighbors because Jesus loves me. I want to share His love with everyone I meet.
- I love and obey my parents and my authorities.
- I love to read the Bible. I know that it is living and active and can change my life.
- I am successful everyday in everything because of Jesus and His finished work on the cross.
- I am the righteousness of God in Christ.
- I am a child of the King—a joint heir with Jesus.

How to have a meaningful daily quiet time

Attitude is everything:
- Come to God with a sense of expectancy and an eagerness to hear from Him.
- Come into His Presence with reverence.
- Ask Him to give you a willingness to obey Him, no matter how He leads you.

Select a specific time:
- Choose the time to read and pray when you are at your best.
- Give God your time and attention.
- Be consistent with the time you set to meet with God.
- If you've not been consistent in the past, start with seven minutes! Everyone can spend seven minutes.

Follow a simple plan that works for you:
- *If you aim at nothing, you will surely hit it.* Have a meaningful plan in place; key word: plan.
- *Relax:* 'Be still and know that He is God.' (Ps. 46:20). Quiet your self before Him.
- *Request:* Pray briefly and ask Him to speak to you: "Search me, O God"; "Open my eyes to see wonderful things in your Word." (Ps. 139:23; Ps. 119:18)
- *Read:* This is where your conversation with God begins. He speaks to you through His Word.
- *Reflect:* Don't rush; meditate on the Scriptures you have read. Journal what you have gleaned.
- *Request:* After the Lord has spoken to you through His Word. Speak to Him in prayer, asking according to things He has revealed.

A simple acrostic to aid in your prayer time:
- **P-Praise the Lord.** Praise God for Who He is; thank Him for His blessings.

- **R-Repent of your sins.** Confess and ask Him to help you turn away from any revealed sin.

- **A-Ask for yourself and others.** Pour out your heart to God in prayer.

- **Y-Yield to God's will.** Reaffirm the Lordship of Jesus Christ in your life, along with your willingness to trust and obey Him.

Your main purpose in having a daily quiet time with the Lord is to get to know Him and to hear from Him. This is not a ritual but a <u>relationship</u> with the living Lord.

A simple suggestion:
- Read the Psalm of the day and every 30th Psalm, completing the entire book of Psalms in one month: Psalm 5, 35, 65, 95, 125.

Works Cited

"The American Colony in Jerusalem, 1870-2006 (A Library of Congress Exhibition)".
    Retrieved December 16, 2015.

The Amplified Bible. Grand Rapids, MI: Zondervan Bible, 1983. Print.

Grant, Terrence. "*The Silence of Unknowing*." Liguori Publications. 1995.

Hawn, C. Michael. *"History of Hymns: "I Surrender All""* Discipleship
    Ministries The United Methodist Church, n.d. Web. 17 Dec. 2015.

Hawn, C. Michael. "*History of Hymns: "Trust and Obey"*" Discipleship
    Ministries The United Methodist Church, n.d. Web. 17 Dec. 2015.

Holy Bible: New International Version. Grand Rapids, MI: Zondervan,
    2005. Print.

Ireland, Michael, "*Veleky Bog: How Great is Our God! The story behind how a
    thunderstorm in Sweden prompted the writing of How Great Thou Art,
    one of Christianity's greatest and much-loved hymns*" ASSIST News
    Service (Sunday, October 7, 2007).

The New Spirit-Filled Life Bible. Nashville, TN: Thomas Nelson Publishers,
    2002. Print.

Peterson, Eugene H. *The Message*. Colorado Springs, CO: NavPress,
    2004. Print.

Strong, James, and James Strong. *The New Strong's Exhaustive Concordance
    of the Bible: With Main Concordance, Appendix to the Main
    Concordance, Key Verse Comparison Chart, Dictionary of the Hebrew
    Bible, Dictionary of the Greek Testament*. Nashville: Thomas Nelson,
    1984. Print.

Voskamp, Ann. "*The Greatest Gift: Unwrapping the Full Love Story of
    Christmas*." Tyndale House Publishers. 2013.

About the Author

Marjie Schaefer was born in Georgia, raised in Texas and has spent the past 3 decades in Washington state. She and her husband, Steve, have been married for over 28 years and have 4 children: daughter Hayley, and sons Jordan, Matthew and Luke.

Marjie describes herself as an everyday girl who loves Jesus and daily pursues a life with Him at the center of her activities and purposes.

She started leading and teaching Bible studies while a student at Washington State University, and has continued to open her home and her life to anyone who wants more of the Word and more of Jesus. Her greatest passion is bringing the Word of God to life through practical application and visual tools. Women look forward to her personal touches while attending her studies, and they usually go home with tangible reminders of God's love for them.

Marjie started spending deliberate and daily time in the Word of God while she was a young girl at the encouragement of her godly mother. This has given her a foundation that has stood the test of time. She began writing her own Bible studies at the request of some friends who desired to study the Word during the summer months.

Marjie and her team currently lead the ministry, **Flourish Through the Word**, which is a community of women in the greater Seattle region committed to being equipped through God's Word. As a result of their time together in the Word, the women move out into their arenas of influence, shining their light for Jesus. You can find out more about this ministry, upcoming events, Bible studies, and the Flourish Conference at www.flourishthroughtheword.com.

Visit the website to sign up for the email and receive regular encouragements from Marjie. Find Flourish on Facebook and 'like' our page. You can also find Marjie on Twitter @followmarjie.

Special Thanks

The study book you hold in your hands is the result of much prayer. Not only that, it is also the fruit of the labor of many hands, and the result of great patience on the part of many others involved in the process.

Thank you to my husband and family who have endured a messy dining room table for weeks on end, along with a few quickly-thrown-together meals so that I could finish the manuscript. I love and appreciate you Steve, Matthew and Luke. (And Hayley and Jordan, but you don't live at home anymore!)

A big thanks is due to Vickie Adair, who researched the hymn stories and did the editing and proof-reading for this study. Vickie also covered this project in prayer.

Thank you too, to Anna Moir, for her part in proof-reading, editing and the final formatting, and getting it to press in a timely manner.

Thank you, Lisa McKenney, for using your talent and gifts to create a stunning cover for us. Thank you, Hannah McKenney, for the beautiful lettering done for our cover page.

Thank you, Katherine Adair for taking the cover photograph of Monreale Cathedral, Monreale, Sicily.

May God use this study for His glory and for the ever-expanding growth of His Kingdom in the lives of His people.

CPSIA information can be obtained
at www.ICGtesting.com
Printed in the USA
FFOW01n1304230117
31681FF